MILNER CRAFT SERIES

Fabric Painting

Raelle Burlak

MILNER

DEDICATION

This book is dedicated to my children Ryan, Melanie, Stephen and Elyse.

First published in 1997 by
Sally Milner Publishing Pty Ltd
RMB 54 Burra Road
Burra Creek New South Wales
Australia 2620

© Raelle Burlak, 1997

Designed by Anna Warren, Warren Ventures, Sydney
Photography by Andrew Elton & Neil Lorimer
Printed and bound by National Capital Printing, Canberra

National Library Cataloguing-in-Publication data:

Burlak, Raelle.
Fabric Painting.

ISBN 1 86351 207 1.

1. Textile painting. I. Title. (Series: Milner craft series).

746.6

Contents

Acknowledgements

There are so many people who have contributed to this book in a lot of big and small ways. Without their help and encouragement, it would not have been possible.

To my children, Ryan, Melanie, Stephen and Elyse, who have all taken on added responsibilities around the house to help out, and for modelling the garments photographed in this book — thanks guys!

To Julie, Shane and family, for the use of the computer and all the help with the bits and pieces.

To Mario for taking the original photographs. To the following children who did a great job modelling: Kayla, Jorden, Morgan, Sally, Matthew, Stacey, Christie, Jodie, Michelle, Hollie and Simone for styling their hair.

Thanks also to Margaret and Judy who tested out the instructions for me. They did a great job. To Pauline and Marj from London Mart, Kilmore, Victoria for their support and guidance.

A WORD FROM
THE AUTHOR

I have taught fabric painting on and off for six years and it has been a big part of my life. When you teach something like fabric painting to many different women, you learn to cater for a variety of styles and tastes — not to mention the problems that arise! In dealing with these situations in class, I feel that I have learned as much from my students as they have from me.

In this book I have covered the most common problems which arise when learning the various fabric painting techniques. Each section deals with a different aspect of fabric painting, for example, transferring, shading, painting tips etc. This way you can apply these methods to any project that you may wish to work on. The instructions are a guide only. If you feel more comfortable approaching certain tasks differently, then do so. Painting is a very personal thing.

Enjoy your painting! That is the most important thing. I hope that you find as much pleasure in painting these designs as I have had in creating them.

As a follow up service to this book, I am providing an address where you can write with any problems regarding your fabric painting. Enclose a stamped, self-addressed envelope with your letter, and make sure to include your telephone number. Send to Raelle Burlak, PO Box 100, Lancefield, Victoria, Australia 3435.

Chapter One

HOW TO USE THIS BOOK

This book has been designed to give you a painting lesson, as if you were sitting in class. All the answers to problems that may arise are here for you. It is important that you read all the sections on the various techniques before attempting the designs, then you will be able to refer to any section as necessary — just like having the teacher at home.

Each chapter deals with a different aspect of fabric painting, including 'Materials and Equipment', 'General Techniques' and 'Painting Techniques'. The final chapter provides detailed step-by-step instructions on how to paint each design.

Within each chapter are different sections, describing in detail specific techniques, such as 'Transferring Patterns', 'Heat-Setting', 'Creating a Colourwash Background' etc. If you are a beginner, I suggest you select one section, for example, 'Shading', 'Highlighting', or 'Outlining', and using a scrap of material, try out the technique with the book open next to you. This will help to give you experience and confidence before starting a full design.

The section, 'Mixing Colours' on page 19, provides instructions on how to mix the most frequently used colours for the designs in this book.

Utilise the information and techniques in this book to paint any design that strikes your fancy. Don't forget to read through all the instructions first. This way you will be familiar with what is required for this design and there will be no surprises!

Adapting the Designs

The designs in this book can be altered to suit personal taste and level of painting skill. The instructions are written so that different sections of the design can be painted individually. Transfer the part of the design that you wish to paint, look up the instructions for that section and start painting. In this way, the design can be made as simple or as complex as you wish.

If the size of the pattern does not suit the garment you have chosen, a photocopier can be used to enlarge or reduce the pattern. Take the garment with you when photocopying to ensure that the correct size is achieved.

Reversing the design can help when trying to place different designs together. Simply trace the pattern with a grey lead pencil first, then turn the tracing over and trace with a transfer pencil on the opposite side. The grey lead will then be facing the iron when you are transferring the design onto your garment.

The colourwash background can be used behind any of the designs, or alternately, the designs pictured with the colourwash background can be painted on a plain-coloured garment.

For example, the 'Teddy Bears' Picnic' design could be painted on white fabric without the colourwash background. Alternately, you might decide to paint the smaller teddies only, rather than the whole scene.

I have two daughters, Melanie, 11, and Elyse, 5. They both wanted a Teddy Bear top, but with the age gap they did not want them to be the same. So, I changed the small bears on the younger girl's top and added balloons, leaving the two larger bears the same on the older girl's top. In this way they had similar, yet different, tops. Melanie's top has a colourwash background (Plate 1-1), while Elyse's was painted on an orange T-Shirt (Plate 1-3). They were delighted with the results.

Chapter Two

MATERIALS AND EQUIPMENT

Paints

I use paints from three different companies: Setacolor from Francheville; Permaset from Colormaker Industries and Scribbles from Duncan's. Unfortunately, no one brand covers all my needs.

Setacolor is a thin free-flowing paint. Permaset, on the other hand, is a thick paint, and I find only three colours in this brand are suitable, as outlined below. Scribbles is a dimensional paint, used to embellish the designs once the other paints have been dried and heat-set. All three brands can be purchased through craft stores.

Permaset and Setacolor paints can be used and mixed together. However, they will only bond together if used when wet. A problem can occur if Setacolor paints are painted over the Permaset paints after the Permaset has dried, as the Setacolor paint can wash off.

Refer to the colour mixing guide on page 19 for instructions on how to mix the colours used most often in this book.

SETACOLOR

Setacolor comes in a great range of colours and three types: Opaque, Transparent and Nacre.

Opaque: The Opaque range can be used successfully on dark coloured fabrics. Usually two or three coats on the dark coloured fabrics will give the desired results. Opaque colours are bright and can be used on light coloured fabrics as well. I tend to use more of this paint than any other.

Transparent: Transparent paints are good on light coloured fabrics but generally can not be used for the darker colours. Even with several coats, the colour will not stand out. I prefer to use the Transparent range for shading flowers and ribbons etc.

Nacre: These are very soft pretty colours with an iridescent look to them. The colours in this range are wonderful for summer tops. However, they are not suitable for dark-coloured fabrics. If you mix Pearl Nacre with any of the Setacolor range you can make your own Nacre colours.

PERMASET

Permaset comes in three types: Supercover, Normal and Metallic.

Supercover: I find the Supercover is just too thick, and needs to be thinned down with Reducer.

Normal: The Normal paint in the Permaset range is rather thick, but the white is great for black and dark coloured fabrics.

Metallic: The two metallic colours that I use from this range are Gold Lustre and Bright Silver. These are also great on dark coloured fabrics and I would not be without them.

DIMENSIONAL PAINTS

The dimensional paints are mainly used for embellishing designs — adding that something special to your garment. They can be used on their own or combined with other paints, which makes them very versatile. These paints do not need heat-setting.

I would not suggest painting a full design, such as the teddy bears, with the dimensional paints as they dry very stiff, making the garment uncomfortable to wear. You can use any brand of dimensional paints that you wish. They all do the same job, some are just easier to use than others.

Most brands have shiny, iridescent and glitter in their range. Scribbles is my preferred brand as the nib is not as wide as other brands, so it does not flow too fast. I use Scribbles paints for decorating gift paper and shoes as well.

Polymark from Polymerics Inc., has a beautiful range of colours which I sometimes use with a brush for different effects. There are so many different uses for this type of paint — the list is endless.

An important point to remember if you are embellishing a painted garment with dimensional paints, is to heat-set your work first. The heat of the iron can actually melt the dimensional paints. Refer to heat-setting instructions on page 16.

TEXTILE MEDIUM

Also known as Incolore, Reducer and Extender, made by both Francheville and Colormaker Industries. Textile Medium is one of the fabric painter's most handy tools. It can be used to remoisten the paint on the tile if it gets a little dry. It can also be used to thin down the paint in the jar if it gets too thick. When shading, the Textile Medium is very handy if the paint starts to dry before you have finished the job. It is a must for every painter's collection.

PUFF PAINTS — PEBEO BROD EXPRESS

The name is self-explanatory: the paint puffs up when heat-set. I like the puff paints in this range because the fine nib allows for some very pretty painting of fine bows, etc.

Most people do not realise that puff paint can be mixed with normal paint. It will lose some of its puffiness, so when painting you need to apply more to compensate.

Puff paint is a great addition to any painting, and can give dimension to your design. One thing to remember if you are going to paint with flat paint (any paint that does not puff up when heat-set) and puff paint on the one design, is to heat-set the flat paint before applying the puff paint. The reason for this is that the flat paint takes three minutes to heat-set and the puff paint takes only one minute approximately. If puff paint is ironed for too long it will flatten. Refer to heat-setting instructions on page 17.

Brushes

SELECTING BRUSHES

Good quality brushes are essential — they last longer and work better. I basically use three different brushes from the Francheville range. Your craft shop will advise you of other good brands if they do not stock these.

The following brushes will help you paint your way through any design:

No. 000 fine brush;

No. 3 round brush;

Flat or chisel-edged brush, approximately 1 cm (½") in width.

Sometimes on a bigger design, a larger brush may be required.

MAINTAINING BRUSHES

Keep your brushes clean and they will last much longer. After a session of painting, wash the brushes well in soapy water. One of my students puts a little dishwashing liquid in the palm of her hand and rolls the hairs of the brush in this, making sure every little bit of paint has been removed, then rinses the brush clean.

Stand the brushes in a clean jar or glass with the hairs pointing upward to prevent the brushes becoming bent. Never leave the brushes sitting in water for any length of time as the hairs will gradually weaken and become bent.

Fabrics

When selecting the material or garment for painting, be careful of cheap synthetic fabrics, as they will quite often scorch when ironing on transfers. A polyester/cotton blend and 100 per cent cotton are ideal.

It is much easier to paint on wind-cheaters or fleecy materials, as opposed to T-Shirts or thinner materials, which tend to move more while you are painting. Also the paint soaks in more quickly, making shading more difficult.

If you are inexperienced, start by painting one or two wind-cheaters before working on T-Shirt fabric. If the grain of the material is too open or thick, it will be more difficult to cover with the paint.

Remember, good quality fabric will always hold you in good stead. You get what you pay for. Do not waste hours of painting on a cheap garment that will not do your work justice.

Note: Always wash your garment or material prior to painting to remove any sizing from the fabric. Do not use fabric softener.

Transfer Pencils

There are many different brands of transfer pencils and pens available. Hobbytex make both transfer pens and pencils in a variety of colours. Birch have their own pencil that comes in pink, but they also sell a brand of pen called Sulky which is made in the USA. These are just a couple of the brands that I use, but most brands will do the same job.

The most important thing to decide is which colour to use when, and do I need a pen as opposed to a pencil? Personally, I prefer the pens as they transfer more quickly and give a stronger transfer, which is particularly helpful if you are a beginner.

If you are doing quite a lot of painting, it would be useful to have a range of pens and pencils in various colours. This way you will be prepared for any job.

(For more details on using transfer pencils, refer to Chapter 3, 'General Techniques'.)

Tracing Paper

Inexpensive greaseproof paper purchased from your local supermarket is the best for transferring patterns. The cheaper the better, and it can be used for other things around the house as well.

For larger designs, tracing paper in large sheets can be purchased from local craft stores. Do not use paper that is waxed or has a greasy feel to it.

Extras

Before starting any of these designs, make sure you are prepared. Following is a list of additional items you may need:

Instructions

Iron

Ironing board

Ironing cloth

Chalk pencil

Sponges for the colourwash background

Rags

Painting tile

Water jar

Detergent for brushes

Cardboard T-Shirt insert

Scotch tape

Pins

Hair dryer

Chapter Three
GENERAL TECHNIQUES

Transferring Patterns

Use the manufacturers instructions for transferring patterns and take note of these pointers to help you achieve a clear transfer.

TIPS FOR TRANSFERRING PATTERNS

Think carefully before ironing on transfers. Placement of the design is important. Try on the garment if necessary to see the best position for the transfer.

Ironing a crease down the centre front of the garment can help with centering the pattern.

To transfer a large design, place several towels or a blanket on the floor or kitchen table. This will provide a larger working area than the ironing board, and may prevent double lines when trying to move the garment around.

Make sure to secure the tracing onto the garment with pins to prevent the paper from moving and giving double lines.

When using the pink or red transfer pencils, a fair amount of pressure needs to be applied when tracing in order for the transfer to iron on clearly.

The lead will need to be sharpened often during tracing as it is soft and will blunt quickly.

Do not move the iron over the paper. Lift and place the iron down, holding it in place for the recommended time, then lift and place the iron on the next section. Repeat until the entire transfer has been completed.

Check to make sure that the pattern has transferred satisfactorily before removing the paper. If any section has not transferred, place the iron over it again.

For transferring smaller designs, kitchen grease-proof paper is inexpensive and works well. When transferring larger designs, I use the large sheets of tracing paper (available from most craft shops). An easy way to work out placement of the larger designs is to trace out the shape of your garment onto tracing paper, then trace the designs onto this shape.

THE NET METHOD

The net method is most effective when transferring patterns on to dark coloured fabrics. Refer to the Step-By-Step photographs.

Place a piece of white or light coloured net over the design you wish to transfer. Trace the design onto the net with a thick black texta. If you wish to keep your design in good order, place a piece of grease-proof paper between the design and the net. Once the design is traced, place the net in position on your garment and secure with pins. With a white chalk pencil or tailor's chalk, trace over the black lines. Remove the net and put aside for the next time you wish to use it. The net can be used many times over.

THE WINDOW METHOD

Another method is to hold the design up against a window and trace over the back of the design with a chalk pencil. Place the picture, chalk-side down, onto the garment and rub over the design with your fingers. Lift the paper off carefully. Be careful not to erase the chalk lines when handling. Refer to the Step-By-Step photograph B.

WHITE AND PASTEL FABRICS

For the lighter coloured fabrics, I prefer to use a pink or red transfer pencil. This way the transferred line is easier to hide with the paint. Yellow and white paint cannot cover the pink or red transfer line, so if you are going to paint with the very pale coloured paints, there is a yellow transfer pen available from Sulky.

TRANSFERRING ONTO DARKER COLOURED FABRICS

For colours such as red, blue and green (as long as the fabric is not too dark), use a blue or dark green transfer pencil. There is also a purple transfer pen from Sulky which is excellent for these darker colours.

TRANSFERRING ONTO BLACK, PURPLE AND BOTTLE GREEN FABRICS

There are a few white transfer pencils on the market, but I find that they do not work very well. The most sure-fire method for transferring designs onto darker coloured fabrics is the net method as explained on page 15.

TRANSFERRING DESIGNS WITH OUTLINES

For designs that need to be outlined such as cartoon characters, I like to transfer with the darker pencils or pens, as the transfer lines will show through the paint making it easier to keep track of where you are going. The black used for outlining will cover the transfer line. A combination of blue and red transfer pencils can be used on the same tracing if you are using a design which has a combination of light and dark colours.

Heat-Setting

This is one of the most important steps in finishing off your painted design, so make sure that it is done properly! If you do not heat-set your garment long enough, you run the risk of the paint washing off. Read the instructions on your paints carefully.

Before starting, make sure the painted garment is completely dry. Leave it in a warm place to dry. I put mine in front of the heater, or in a sunny position in the house. A great idea is to leave the garment in a car parked in the sun.

METHOD

For the brands of paint recommended in this book, I use an old white or cream-coloured pillow slip that has been cut open, and place it over the dry painted area.

Iron over the cloth on a wool/cotton setting for three minutes. If it is a large design, the rule is: whatever fits on the ironing board gets ironed for three minutes. Then, move the iron to the next section of the garment, and iron for a further three minutes. It may take nine to 12 minutes to heat-set a large design. An ironing press can also be used, but test on a sample piece first.

HEAT-SETTING PERMASET PAINTS

When thicker paints, such as Permaset, have been used, the paint can take a long time to dry. Sometimes in the cooler weather it may still feel tacky after one or two weeks. If the paint feels tacky (even after this amount of time), do not heat-set it. I have known several women who attempted to heat-set, thinking the paint must be dry. The result: the paint has peeled off onto the ironing cloth.

If you find that the paint is sticking to the cloth, continue ironing until the cloth comes away easily. The heat of the iron will dry the paint through. However, it is much easier to avoid this in the first place.

For more information on Permaset paints, refer to page 9.

HEAT-SETTING PUFF PAINT

When heat-setting puff paint, I use the same method, except that puff paint is not ironed for three minutes. Generally, one minute should do. When the paint is puffed up, it is heat-set. Do not continue to iron, as over-ironing will flatten the puff paint.

For more information on puff paint, refer to page 10.

DIMENSIONAL PAINTS

An important point to remember if you are embellishing a painted garment with dimensional paints, is to heat-set your work first as the heat of the iron will melt the dimensional paints.

I have had a few students who have forgotten to heat-set their work first. I must admit I have done it myself. If this does happen, heat-set the entire design when it is dry, for one minute at a time. In other words, heat-set for one minute, remove the ironing cloth and allow it to cool down, then repeat until the normal paints have been heat-set for the correct amount of time.

For more information on dimensional paints, refer to page 9.

Chapter Four

PAINTING TECHNIQUES

Mixing Colours

If I can mix a colour rather than buying it, I do. Once you get past that mental barrier about mixing colours, a whole new world of colours will open up for you. By mixing paints in an air-tight jar or container, they will last for weeks, and in some cases, months.

Listed below are some of the most common colour combinations that I use. The colours may vary between different brands of paint, and in the following examples, I have used Setacolor paints. Remember that the colours will dry between one to two shades darker.

FLESH
Add 2 parts white to 1 part red, to make a soft pink, then add 1 brush of yellow. The yellow will tone down the pink to give that flesh appearance.

GREY
Add 2 parts white to 1 part black. The more black you add the darker the grey will become.

CREAM
Add 2 parts white to 1 part gold (nacre or metallic is suitable).

ORANGE
Add 2 parts yellow to 1 part red. This will give you more of a buttercup colour, as it is difficult to get a true orange when mixing.

GOLDEN BROWN
Add 2 parts gold to 1 part brown.

AQUAMARINE
Add 1 part blue, to 1 part green, to 2 parts silver or pearl.

RAW SIENNA
Add 6 parts orange, to 2 parts red, to 1 part brown.

COPPER
Add 2 parts gold to 1 part Sienna (opaque).

MISSION BROWN (CHAMOIS)
Add 2 parts brown to 1 part black.

EMERALD GREEN
Add 1 part yellow to 2 parts dark blue.

MOSS GREEN
Add 2 parts yellow to 1 part dark blue.

OLIVE GREEN
Add 2 parts yellow, to 1 part dark blue, plus a touch of black.

FAWN
Add 1 part brown, to 1 part yellow, to 1 part white.

WISTERIA
Add 1 part purple, to 1 part blue, to 1 part white.

To create a pastel shade, just add enough white to any colour. To mute a colour (used when an old-fashioned touch is needed), add a touch of black or brown.

Adding Pearl or Bright Silver (metallic) to any colour will give it an iridescent or metallic look. Mix silver with cool colours and gold with warm colours.

Shading

Shading can make a world of difference to your painting. It will turn a plain picture into a work of art to be truly proud of. With a little practise, shading can be mastered. It takes very little extra time or effort.

A common reason for shading, is to show that an object is in the background or in shadow. For example, I would shade under the Teddy Bear's chin to separate the face from the body. Also the background arm or leg should be shaded with a darker colour for emphasis. Refer to the Step-By-Step photographs I and J.

BRUSHES

The most important thing is to use a good quality brush. I find that the No. 3 round brush from Francheville is good for the majority of shading tasks. It is soft enough so that the hairs spread slowly and gently, moving the paint with ease. If the hairs on the brush are too hard or brittle, they will push the paint through the fabric creating a patchy look when the paint is dry. Use the size brush for each area of painting that you feel most comfortable using.

SHADING TIPS

Refer to Step-By-Step photographs I and J which show the boy teddy bear being painted and the girl teddy bear's face being painted.

If applying more than one coat of paint, shading should only be done on the last coat.

The base colour that you are shading into must be fairly wet. This allows the paints to blend into each other to give a subtle colour change. Shading is just like applying cheek blush!

The colour should be subtle with no definite cut-off line. The most common shading is the blushing of cheeks, so this is a good point to remember.

As soon as you have applied the base colour, paint a few dots or strokes of the colour with which you wish to shade. Wash and dry the brush, then gently blend in the colour. You may need to wash and dry your brush again to remove any excess colour, then continue to blend in the colour. If the shading is not dark enough, more colour can be added.

The base paint must be fairly wet, so bear this in mind when covering a large area. Shade as you go along. You will soon learn how much time you have before the paint is too dry to shade successfully. If the paint does dry too much, go over the base paint with a little Textile Medium (also known as Incolor, Extender, Reducer). This will re-moisten the base. Do not use water as this can make the paint bleed.

On the other extreme, sometimes the base colour can be too wet to shade into. The brand of paint being used and the room temperature can have a bearing on this. If the base is too wet, the colour being shaded in will virtually disappear into the base colour. Just allow a few minutes for it to dry a little, then try again.

When shading, I find the results are much better if the paint is not being patted. A longer sweeping stroke is generally better. However, this will of course depend on the area being shaded. For example, when painting a balloon, I sweep the brush around the edge of the circle taking in half or more of the balloon with a single stroke. The brush rarely lifts off the balloon until it is finished. Refer to the Step-By-Step photograph O.

With something like gathering on a dress, the strokes are vertical — a single stroke starting at the top, then brought downward in one sweeping movement. Reload your brush and repeat until all gathers are done. Experiment and have a play. You will soon have a professional look.

A light touch is important. If you are too heavy handed, the brush will push the paint through the base colour to the material and this will result in the paint drying blotchy.

When shading, always use a small amount of paint at a time. You know the old saying: 'It is easier to add than to take away'. But remember, there is not much that cannot be fixed. If for example, your teddy bear looks like it has a 104-degree temperature rather than a lovely blush, don't panic! Use a clean, dry brush to lift off the excess colour, then gently blend down the paint again. If you have scraped off too much paint, then apply more base colour and re-apply the blush again.

COLOURS USED FOR SHADING

Any colour that is deeper than the base colour can be

used for shading. Generally Setacolor Chamois (opaque) or Black Noir are used to shade any area that is in the background or in shadow.

Chamois is a very dark brown, but if you do not have this colour, any dark brown or mixture of equal parts black and brown will do.

For fairies, gum-nut babies or any design with a flesh base, the Black Noir or Chamois will be too heavy for shading. I like to use a mixture of equal parts Setacolor Brown Velvet (opaque) and Setacolor Cherry (opaque). It gives a much softer, prettier effect. Any shade of red can be used for blushing — whatever you have in your painting box will do.

Most of the opaque colours in the Setacolor range have a 'colour mate' in the transparent range from the same company. For example, Bengal Rose (opaque) has Fuchsia (transparent), and Light Green (opaque) has Emerald Green (transparent). The beauty of this is that if you are painting with Bengal Rose (transparent), you can shade with the Fuchsia (transparent) as it is much darker.

If you have mixed a pastel colour using, for instance, Parma Violet (opaque) and White to make mauve, then shade with Parma Violet. The same would apply to any mixed colour, even if three or more colours are involved.

Highlighting

Highlighting is treated the same as shading, except that it gives the opposite effect.

COLOURS USED FOR HIGHLIGHTING

A colour lighter than the base colour is used, and white is the colour most commonly used. However, a nice effect can be achieved when Setacolor Pearl (nacre) or Permaset Bright Silver (metallic) is used to highlight cool colours, and Setacolor Gold (nacre) or Permaset Gold Lustre is used to highlight warm colours. This gives you the option of many different looks. Try them out and see for yourself! Refer to the

Step-by-Step photograph C of Navy Highlighting.

The transparent colours in the Setacolor range lend themselves beautifully to being highlighted with white. Try painting a bow in Fuchsia (transparent), then highlight the front of the bow and the curve of the ribbon in white, leaving the inside of the bow and the ribbon just under the bow, untouched. The results are very pretty! Refer to the Step-By-Step photograph D of the Fuchsia Bow.

Outlining

This is the part that makes most people nervous! Outlining can be a bit daunting at first, but with some practise and a few tricks of the trade, you will surprise yourself.

PAINT

An important factor with outlining is the paint. It must be fairly thin so that it can be easily and smoothly moved. Setacolor paint is ideal for outlining because of its consistency. If you only have a thicker brand of paint, thin the paint with Textile Medium (also known as Reducer, Incolor and Extender). Do not use water to thin the paint, as this will make the paint bleed on the material.

BRUSHES

Make sure you have a fine brush, anything from a No. 0 to a No. 000 will do. The thicker the brush, the thicker the outline will be. I personally keep one fine brush just for outlining and painting eyes. If kept aside just for this purpose, you will be assured of a nice fine point on your brush. Use the size brush for each area of painting that you feel most comfortable using.

OUTLINING TIPS

I prefer to outline on the very edge of the paint rather than on the fabric. This gives a smoother, more consistent line and there is also less chance of the outline bleeding. Refer to close-up of brush outlining in Step-By-Step photograph E.

Do not try to outline with your hand up in the air. Place your hand as close to the area that you are outlining as you can. Rest the edge of your hand on the garment or table. I prefer to outline the design as it is being painted, to avoid smudging the paint while working. Turn the garment around to suit the angle of your hand.

A small amount of paint, just on the tip of the brush is all that is needed. The more paint on the brush, the thicker the line will be. It is better to reload the brush more often, outlining small sections at a time.

Try to keep the strokes even and don't apply too much pressure to the brush. I use only half way up the hairs of the brush when outlining. If you push too hard on the brush, the hairs will be forced to spread making the line too thick.

If outlining with a different brand of paint than the base colour, make sure that the outline is done while the base paint is still wet to avoid the outline washing off. This can be the case when using Setacolor over Permaset as I do in this book. Remember this rule and all will be fine.

Painting Eyes

A first pointer: do not transfer on the eyelashes. The reason for this is that the transfer pencil will, more often than not, show through the paint when it dries. Using a paint brush will give a much thinner line than using the pencil. Refer to the Step-By-Step photograph F of eyes and mouth being painted.

STEP-BY-STEP INSTRUCTIONS

When painting eyes, block the complete eye with white paint, then shade the colour that you are using for the iris, leaving the colour heavier towards the edge.

Dab in the black pupil, wash and dry the brush,

then gently blend in the outer edge of the black pupil so that there is no definite line.

Pick up a little white paint on a fine brush and dab on to one side of the eye. If the white is too definite use a clean, dry brush and blend it in a little.

Outline the eye with black or Chamois. If the outline is too thick or crooked, allow to dry a little then touch it up with white.

Now paint the eyelashes. Use the very tip of a No. 000 brush for a nice fine line. Put a little black paint on the very tip of the brush and push the brush down ever so slightly at the base of the eyelash, lifting the brush off as you paint towards the end of the lash. This will thin the lash nicely. Make sure to curve the lashes the right way and be careful not to cross the eyes. This is actually a very common mistake. Just take a second to make sure you are doing it correctly. It is like anything that is worthwhile, practice makes perfect.

Painting Mouths

Refer to the Step-By-Step photograph F of eyes and mouth being painted.

STEP-BY-STEP INSTRUCTIONS

The easiest way to paint mouths is to paint two small daubs of paint for the top half of the mouth and a larger daub for the bottom of the mouth.

Highlight the centre area with a little white paint, then blend this in a little.

Place a small amount of black in the centre with a line going to the sides of the mouth.

With a clean dry brush, take the sharpness off the edge of the black paint by blending in the edges very gently.

Creating a Colourwash Background

This is an interesting and pretty way to add background colour to your design. I once priced bottles of spray-on paints which provide the same effect as this technique. They were $10.00 per bottle. It would have cost me $40.00 before I even started. With this method you can use up any seemingly empty bottles of paint lying in the bottom of your paint box, and the colours are only limited by your imagination, not your budget.

I prefer to use transparent colours, as they are more subtle when used this way. If you are using opaque paints only half the amount of paint is required as the colours are much stronger. Dimensional paints such as Scribbles and Polymark can be used if colouring a small area only. The paints dry quite stiff which is not very comfortable to wear.

I have used the colourwash background for the 'Teddy Bears' Picnic' design as an example for this technique. Refer to the Step-By-Step photographs G and H of the colourwash background.

MATERIALS NEEDED

Plastic to line the inside of the garment

Rubber gloves

Water spray bottle

Foam brush (available from craft supply shops), or pieces of kitchen sponge, one for each colour

Clean containers, one for each colour (Chinese take-away containers are best)

PAINTS

Setacolor Emerald (transparent), Lemon Yellow (opaque), Ultramarine Blue (transparent), Parma Violet (transparent) is optional.

PREPARATION

If you have bought your garment, line the inside with the plastic. The front must be colourwashed first, then left to dry, before the back is painted (if you want to do the back). If you are sewing the garment yourself, join the front and back at the shoulder seams and sew in the sleeves, leaving the side seams open so that it can be laid open on a table to be painted. I like to sew in the neck rib as well.

MIXING THE PAINTS

Mix 1 teaspoon of Emerald Green with water to make approximately 1 cup. Add a small amount of water only at first to avoid lumps, then gradually add the rest. Make sure the paint is mixed well. Repeat for all colours. Do not forget to only use a half teaspoon of paint if using opaque paints.

STEP-BY-STEP INSTRUCTIONS

Using the water spray bottle, spray the garment all over with clean water until it is quite damp.

Saturate a piece of the kitchen sponge in the Emerald Green water and rub onto the bottom of the garment. Continue to dip the sponge in the paint and repeat until the area indicated is covered.

Next apply the Lemon Yellow water to the right shoulder area in a sun-burst shape.

Apply the Ultramarine Blue water over the left shoulder, bringing it right down to the Emerald. With the butt of your hand rub over the area joining the green and blue paints so that there is no definite line between them.

Take the blue in between the yellow sunburst, being careful not to take over the yellow paint.

If you wish you can put some of the purple water over the blue on the shoulder and down the back. This is optional but has a pretty effect.

FINISHING

When you are happy with the results, allow the paint to dry. It is a good idea to heat-set the colourwash background before transferring on the design, just in case of any little mishaps. Refer to heat-setting instructions on page 16.

TIPS FOR CREATING A COLOURWASH BACKGROUND

The paint will fade a little when dry, so keep this in mind when applying the colour.

If you are applying the colourwash background to the front of the garment only, then spray less water toward the sides. If the paint is spreading to the wrong places, then dry it with a hairdryer. The wetter the garment, the quicker and further the paint will spread. The dryer it is, the slower the paint will spread.

The best method is to lie your garment out to dry on a trampoline. If the weather is not good, lie the garment on plastic on the floor in front of the heater. Do not hang it over a clothes line or airer to dry, as the colours will run down the garment.

If you are not happy with the colour when dry, the process can be repeated. More paint or more water, whichever the case may be, can be added as needed.

One problem which can occur is watermark lines, but this can be easily overcome by positioning the clouds or butterflies over the mark to disguise it.

The outcome of the colourwash background is totally unpredictable. That is what is so great about it. Each one is different, an individual piece of work.

General Painting Tips

There will always be times when you get into trouble. Just remember, when something goes wrong, there is always a way round it. Keep a level head and don't panic. Take a minute to work out the best solution.

Here are a few ways to avoid trouble in the first place:

- Make sure you have a piece of cardboard inside the garment, large enough to cover the area that you are painting. Some craft shops sell T-Shirt boards which are ideal for this.

- Do not cover the cardboard with plastic unless you are doing a colourwash background. The plastic will make the paint spread back through the garment.

- Use pegs to secure the garment on the cardboard. Pin the sleeves back out of the way if necessary.

- If you are a messy painter, it is a good idea to place a few clean rags on the garment, around the area that you are painting. That way the rags will get dirty instead of the garment if you spill anything.

- Use the largest brush possible for the area that you are painting.

- Always wash and dry brushes before starting to paint.

- Have everything you need close at hand, such as paints, brushes, rags, water, instructions, hairdryer etc.

- Do not allow paint to spread beyond the ferrule (metal part) of the brush. It is better to re-load your brush more often to avoid this mess.

- Keep your hands clean.

- Paint onto the transfer line. Do not leave the line showing beyond the edge of the paint. This will give a more professional look.

- It only takes a few strokes to use up the paint on your brush. Do not keep painting if there is no paint left on the brush. Reload frequently. You will notice that it is actually quicker in the long run.

- Try not to paint near the edge of the design first. Start painting near the middle, just in case the paint bleeds. If the paint is bleeding, load the brush with less paint when painting close to the edge. A hairdryer will dry the paint and stop it bleeding, if you need to use it.

- When washing your brush between colours, make sure both the hairs and the handle are completely dry. Sometimes, just one drop of water, further up the handle, will roll down onto the hairs unexpectedly, and make a nice mess of your painting.

- If your fabric is thin, it will quite often stick to the cardboard as the paint dries. Lift the garment up a few times during painting to avoid this. If it is too late, pull the garment off the cardboard. Any paper stuck to the inside of the garment will come off in the first wash.

- If you are right-handed, start painting from the top left-hand side of the design. Vice versa for left-handed folk. This will prevent your arm landing in the paint.

- Do not wear loose-sleeved tops or bracelets when painting. They can make a right mess.

- When applying a second coat of colour, the first coat needs to be three-quarters to fully dry. A hairdryer can speed up the drying process.

- You can always cover up any spilled bits of paint with your signature, or an extra flower, or butterfly — the list is endless.

- Do not be too critical of your work. Go away from your painting or stand back from it. It will always look better after a break.

LIST OF STEP-BY-STEP PHOTOGRAPHS

LIST OF COLOUR PLATES OF PROJECTS

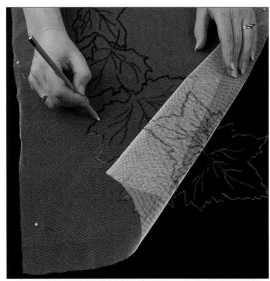

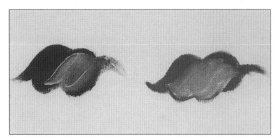

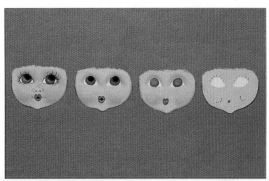

Top left: A: Paints and brushes

Top right: B: Net Method of transferring patterns

Above: C: Navy highlighting

Left: D: Fuchsia Bow

Below left: E: Close-up of brush outlining

Below: F: Eyes and mouth being painted

Above: G: Colourwash background being applied

Above: H: Colourwash background with transferred pattern

Below: I: Girl Teddy's face being painted

Below: J: Boy Teddy being painted

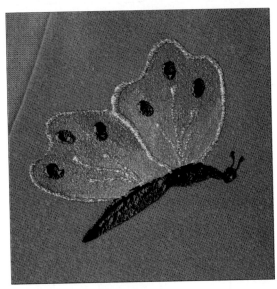

K: Wishing well and Teddy with parasol (close-up back)

L: Close-up of butterfly

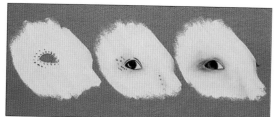

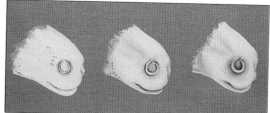

Above: M: Eye being painted
Below: O: Balloons being painted

Above: N: Nostril being painted
Below: P: Frog being painted

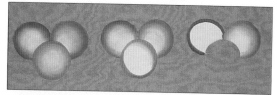

Above: Q: Close-up of reclining frog and frog's head with flower (on side of top)
Below: S: Close-up of peacock

Above: R: Autumn leaves (unfinished)
Below: T: Fairy and fairy dress being painted

1.1 Teddy Bears' Picnic: front view on colourwash background

Top: 1.2 Teddy Bears' Picnic: back view with wishing well
Below: 1.3 Teddy Bears' Picnic: front view with balloons on orange T-Shirt

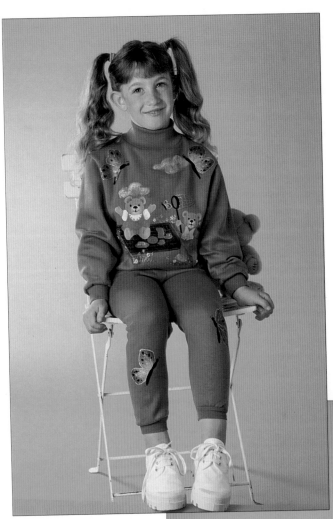

Left: 1.4 Teddy Bears' Picnic:
front view of mauve tracksuit

Below: 1.5 Teddy Bears' Picnic:
girl Teddy floating with Father
Teddy on grey top

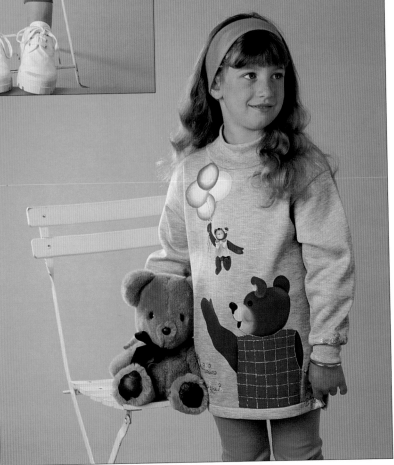

Above left: 2.1 Unicorn head with castle, rainbow and background mist on mauve top

Above right: 2.2 Small unicorn with castle and rainbow on purple top

2.3 Unicorn head on musk top

2.4 Small unicorn on black top

Above: 3.1 Circus Clowns on red top: front view
Below: 3.2 Circus Clowns on red top: back view with elephant

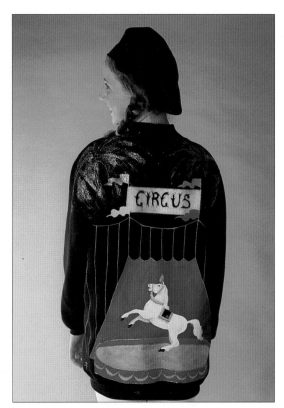

Above left: 3.3 Circus Clowns on black top with hat: front view
Above right: 3.4 Circus Clowns on black top: back view with rearing horse
Below left: 3.5 Circus Clowns on mauve tracksuit: front view
Below right: 3.6 Circus Clowns on mauve tracksuit: back view with elephant

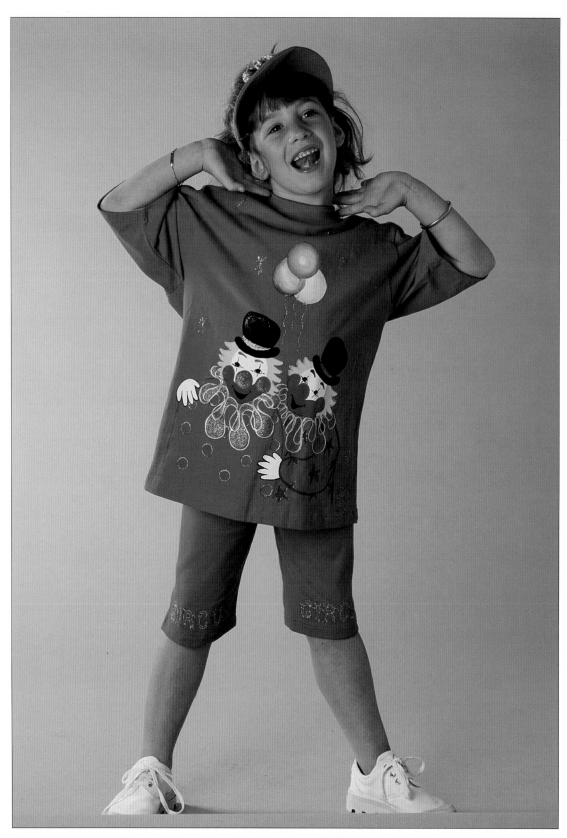

3.7 Circus Clowns: aqua shorts and T-Shirt set with visor

Above: 4.1 Frogs in a Pond on colourwash background: front view
Below: 4.2 Frogs in a Pond on colourwash background: back view with frog fishing

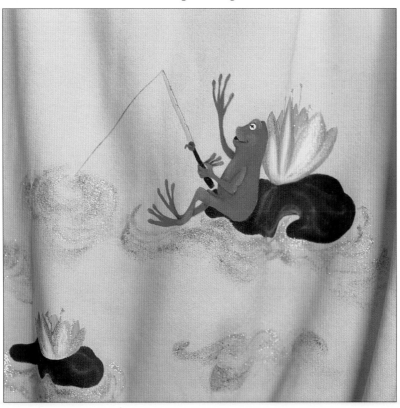

4.3 Frogs in a Pond: variation

Right: 5.1 Dragon: front view

Below: 5.2 Dragon: back view

6 Giraffe

Above: 7 Autumn Leaves
Below: 8 Peacock

Left: 9.1 Mushrooms and Toad-stools with Fairy: front view

Below: 9.2 Hat and Shoes

Chapter Five
FABRIC PAINTING PROJECTS

This chapter explains step-by-step how to paint each design. The instructions for each design include a list of the paints and brushes you will need, a detailed explanation of how to paint each picture, as well as a reminder of how to prepare and finish each garment. Refer back to the sections on transferring patterns, painting techniques and heat-setting when necessary.

Teddy Bears' Picnic

(Plate 1: 1-5)

This design is one of my favourites. I adore teddies — they seem to bring out the child in all of us. This design was actually created for a friend, Claire, who is absolutely obsessed with teddy bears. I hope that you get as much pleasure out of these precious bears as we have.

enlarge as required

PAINTS

Setacolor Brown Velvet (opaque), Black Noir (opaque), Cherry (opaque), Parma Violet (opaque), Lemon Yellow (opaque), Gold (nacre), Green Moss (transparent), Cobalt Blue (opaque), Light Green (opaque), Bengal Rose (opaque); Permaset White

Note: If painting on a light coloured fabric, use Brown Velvet (opaque). If painting on a darker coloured fabric, mix White and Gold (nacre) into the Brown Velvet until you have the desired colour. Remember that the paint will dry a few shades darker.

BRUSHES

Choose the size brush for each area of painting that you feel most comfortable using: No. 3 round brush, No. 000 fine brush, chisel-edged brush.

PREPARATION

Make sure to have all the necessary equipment at hand. Wash your garment prior to painting to remove any sizing from the fabric. Do not use fabric softener. Enlarge or reduce the pattern as required, and transfer the design. Refer to the instructions for transferring patterns on page 14.

GIRL TEDDY ON PICNIC RUG
(Plate 1-1, I)

Refer to Step-By-Step photograph I of girl teddy's face being painted.

Head: Using the No. 3 round brush, paint the head and ears in Brown Velvet. Make sure to paint round the eyes and muzzle. Highlight inside the ears with White. Paint the muzzle in White, going around the nose and mouth. Wash and dry the brush, then blend the Brown Velvet paint from the face into the White using a circular movement. This will give a beige tint to the White paint and take away the definite line between the Brown Velvet and White. Blush the cheeks with a little Cherry, then paint in the eyes, nose and mouth with Black Noir, using the No. 000 fine brush.

Body: Paint the arms in Brown Velvet and highlight the top of the hands with White. Next paint the body and legs with Brown Velvet, highlighting the top of the feet and around the belly with White.

Paint the yoke and sleeves of the dress with White, then shade the folds in the sleeves with Parma Violet. (It may be useful to dry the brown paint with a hairdryer first to avoid the brown smudging into the white.) Paint the flowers around the yoke with Parma Violet, using the No. 000 fine brush. Paint five or six dots in a circle to form a flower, then paint a Lemon Yellow dot in the centre of the flower. Repeat until the yoke is ringed with flowers.

Paint the dress in Parma Violet, paint the folds of the dress in White and shade the underpart of the skirt with Black Noir. Paint the hair bow in Parma Violet, highlighting the front of the bow with White.

Picnic Rug: Paint the rug White, making sure to go around the jug and plates. Using Cherry, paint vertical and horizontal lines to make the checks. Paint the border of the rug with Cherry. Paint the jug, cups and plates with Lemon Yellow, and the cake with Brown Velvet.

BOY TEDDY ON PICNIC RUG
(Plate 1-1, J)

Refer to Step-By-Step photograph J of boy teddy being painted.

Head: Refer to instructions for 'Girl Teddy' above.

Body: Paint the arms and neck with Brown Velvet. Highlight the top of the hands with White, and shade under the chin and armpits with Black Noir. Paint the legs in Brown Velvet, shading the top near the pants with Black Noir. Highlight the feet and front leg with White. Paint the overalls with Lemon Yellow. Allow to dry, then apply a second coat. Using the No. 000 fine brush, shade the creases with Black Noir. Finally, paint the buttons with Black Noir.

Teddy Bear's Picnic

enlarge as required

MOTHER TEDDY
(Plate 1-1)

Hat: Mix 2 parts Gold to 1 part Brown Velvet to make Golden Brown. Paint the hat with this. Shade behind the flowers and background of the hat rim with Brown Velvet. Highlight the crown and rim with Gold. Paint the leaves in Green Moss, highlighting one side of each leaf with White.

To paint the roses, mix 3 parts White to 1 part Cherry on a tile. Apply the paint thickly, then using the back end of the brush, indent a swirl in the paint. Load the No. 000 fine brush with Cherry, and lightly paint over the swirls.

Head: Paint the face using the instructions for 'Girl Teddy' above. Highlight the eyes and nose with White.

Body and Bow: Paint the neck with Brown Velvet, shading under the chin with Black Noir. Paint the sleeves in White, shading the gathers with Parma Violet. Paint the dress with Parma Violet. Shade the areas under the ribbon with Black Noir. Use the left-over paint from the roses to paint the bow. Highlight the front of the bow, the bottom of the ribbon and the sides of the ribbon around the face with White. If needed, shade under and inside the bow with Cherry.

FATHER TEDDY
(Plate 1-1)

Head: Paint with Brown Velvet, leaving the eye and muzzle for later. Shade below the front ear, background ear and base of head with Black Noir. Highlight the front of the ear with White. Paint the muzzle and inside the ear with White, then blend the Brown Velvet from the face over the White with a clean dry brush (refer to instructions for 'Girl Teddy' above). Apply cheek blush using Cherry. Paint the nose, eye and mouth with Black Noir, using the No. 000 brush for the finer lines. Highlight the eye and nose with White.

Body: Paint the arms in Brown Velvet, highlighting the

top of the hand with White. Shade the area near the vest with Black Noir. Paint the vest in Cobalt Blue. Allow to dry and apply a second coat.

WISHING WELL AND GIRL TEDDY WITH PARASOL
(Plate 1-2, K)

Refer to Step-By-Step photograph K showing close-up of wishing well and teddy with parasol.

Well: Paint the timberwork on the roof and posts with White. Shade where indicated with Green Moss. Paint the roof in Green Moss, highlighting the corners with White. To paint the bluestones, mix equal parts Black Noir and Cobalt Blue, then add a brushload of White. Paint each brick one by one, highlighting the bottom of each brick with White as you go. Paint the inside of the well with Black Noir.

To paint the teddy's face, refer to the instructions for 'Girl Teddy' above. Then paint the hands with

enlarge as required

Brown Velvet, highlighting the tops with White. Paint the hat in Parma Violet and Light Green.

Girl Teddy with Parasol: To paint the teddy, refer to instructions for 'Girl Teddy' above. Paint the parasol using equal parts Bengal Rose and White. Paint the lines of the parasol in Bengal Rose, blending in the very edge of the line with a clean dry brush. Shade under the fringe with Bengal Rose. Paint the fringe with White. Using the No. 000 fine brush, shade lines down the fringe with Bengal Rose. Be careful not to overdo it.

Use the remainder of the pink paint (already mixed) to paint the dress. Shade the fold lines from the yoke down the dress with the No. 000 fine brush, using Bengal Rose. Paint the yoke, sleeves, hem and pantaloons with White, and shade with Bengal Rose.

Paint the parasol handle with Black Noir. Paint the coin with grey, using a mixture of Black Noir and White. (Alternately, use silver paint if you have any.)

CLOUDS

Load White paint onto a large brush, dab off the excess, then lightly paint clouds with a swirling movement. Shade the bottom half of the clouds with a small amount of Cobalt Blue.

EXTRA DESIGNS

I have included extra patterns such as the teddies floating with balloons. Refer to the photograph of the grey top (Plate 1-5) and orange top (Plate 1-3).

To paint these, follow the instructions for the 'Girl Teddy' on page 34, and the 'Boy Teddy' on page 37, using the photographs as a guide.

Please note: The 'Father Teddy' pictured on the grey windcheater (Plate 1-5) is painted only on the front. Some of the other designs have the 'Father Teddy' wrapping around the back. Patterns are included for both of these.

The instructions for painting the balloons are included with the Circus Clown design on page 49.

FINISHING

The garment should be left to dry for as long as possible, then heat-set as described on page 16. Once heat-set, the fun begins adding the areas of the design which require dimensional paints.

ADDING DIMENSIONAL PAINTS

The dimensional paints used for this design are from the Scribbles range, but do not rush out and buy the colours I have used. Look in your paint collection and use whatever you have. The colours used here are intended only as a guide. Refer to page 9 for further information on dimensional paints.

Butterfly: (Refer to Step-By-Step photograph L for close-up of butterfly). Colours used: Scribbles Shiny Black, Shiny Bright Yellow, Shiny Purple, Shiny Light Pink, Scribbles Iridescent Golden Brown, Iridescent Shamrock Green, Iridescent Watermelon, Iridescent Golden Turquoise, Scribbles Glittering Crystal, Glittering Amethyst, Glittering Starlight Rose, Glittering Aquamarine, Glittering Gold, Glittering Silver.

Transfer butterflies where desired. Squeeze Iridescent Watermelon on the inside of the wings nearest the body. Brush the paint out with the chisel-edged brush to cover approximately half the wing. Squeeze Glittering Starlight Rose along the outside edge of the wing and brush inwards until the glitter meets the Watermelon paint. Take the glitter just over the other paint to ensure there is no definite line left. Don't cover the entire wing with glitter. Repeat for the other wing. Using Glittering Silver, paint the veins and outline the wings. Paint the dots on the wings and body in Shiny Black.

The other butterflies can be painted in any combination. For example, Shiny Purple with Glittering Amethyst, Iridescent Golden Turquoise with Glittering Crystal, Shiny Bright Yellow with Glittering Gold.

Butterfly Net: Paint the stick with Shiny Black and the net with Iridescent Golden Brown.

Sun: Squeeze Glittering Gold around the face of the

sun and down the rays. Brush this paint down. Outline the face and sunrays with Shiny Bright Yellow.

Jug, Plates and Cake: Outline the jug, cups and plates with Shiny Bright Yellow. Outline the cake in Iridescent Golden Brown.

Grass: The background of the grass is brushed over with Glittering Crystal. The grass is painted with Iridescent Shamrock Green. Move the nib of the paint bottle over the material, as if you are scribbling a message but don't know how to write.

Flowers: The flowers are painted by squeezing dots of paint in a circle, usually five dots to a flower. Colours used here are Iridescent Watermelon, Shiny Light Pink with Shiny Bright Yellow centres, but any pretty colours will do.

GLITTER (OPTIONAL)

Brush Glittering Crystal on clouds, bows, Mother Teddy's sleeves, the flowers on her hat, the roof of the wishing well and the parasol. Father Teddy's vest looks great with checks painted in Glittering Aquamarine.

Unicorn Fantasy

(Plate2: 1-4)

PAINTS

Setacolor Chamois (opaque), Black Noir (opaque), Ultramarine Blue (transparent), Parma Violet (opaque), Lemon Yellow (opaque), Bengal Rose (opaque), Cobalt Blue (opaque), Brown Velvet (opaque), Permaset White.

BRUSHES

Choose the size brush for each area of painting that you feel most comfortable using: No. 3 round brush, No. 000 fine brush, chisel-edged brush.

Unicorn Fantasy

enlarge as required

PREPARATION

Make sure to have all the necessary equipment at hand.

Wash the garment prior to painting to remove any sizing from the fabric. Do not use fabric softener. Enlarge or reduce the pattern as required, and transfer the design. Refer to the instructions for transferring patterns on page 14.

BACKGROUND MIST

After transferring the design, lightly dampen the area where the mist is to be applied using a water spray bottle. Pick up a little Permaset White paint with a large brush, tap the excess onto a rag and very lightly apply the paint using a swirling movement. If the paint is too strong, spray it with a little more water. Wash and dry the brush, then continue to gently blend in the paint.

UNICORN HEAD

(Plate 2-1 and 2-3)

Ears: Using the chisel-edged brush, paint the inside ear with White, shade with Chamois. Paint the rest of the ear with White. Using a clean dry brush, blend the outline of the inner ear to prevent a definite line remaining. Shade in a small amount of Black Noir at the base of the inner ear. Repeat with second ear.

Face: Paint the unicorn's face to just below the eye area with White. Shade under the ear and around the eye with Chamois, blending it in well.

Eye: (Refer to the Step-By-Step photograph M of eye being painted.) Paint the eye White then paint a thin line, using the No. 000 fine brush, around the eye with Black Noir. Blend this in gently with a soft clean brush, moving the paint around the eye and dragging the colour approximately 2 cm (⅘") out from the eye. If you lose the black shading, re-apply the colour and start again. Colour the eye ball with Black Noir, shading a small amount of White to one side of the eye. Using the No. 000 fine brush, paint the eyelashes with Black Noir.

Continue the White paint down the rest of the face, leaving the centre of the nostril blank.

Nostril and Mouth: (Refer to the Step-By-Step photograph N of nostril being painted.) Shade the cheek area and around the nostril with Chamois. When satisfied with the colour, shade a little Black Noir around the nostril as well.

Paint a line with Black Noir for the mouth, and with a clean dry brush, blend in the edge of the black slightly. Paint the inside of the nostril with White, and shade the bottom half of the nostril with Black Noir.

Before painting the neck, make sure that the face has the desired look. It is not too late to add more colour to your shading.

Neck and Mane: Paint the Unicorn's neck and mane with White. Shade under the cheek with Chamois. Using the Ultramarine Blue and the No. 3 round brush, paint in the lines of the mane using the transfer lines as a guide. Gently blend in the blue paint using long sweeping strokes. Do the same with the forelock. Place strokes of Parma Violet randomly between the blue curls of the mane and forelock. Blend in lightly. If the blue and violet become too dark, re-apply white over the top.

Horn: Paint the horn with White. Shade over the transferred lines with Chamois, then, with a clean dry brush, blend in the very edge of the Chamois.

RAINBOW
(Plate 2-1 and 2-2)

Paint the yellow line of the rainbow first. It is best to paint the lighter colours first to prevent them picking up the darker colours. Continue to paint the other lines with the rest of the colours. Make sure the colours are painted close together. Take a clean, slightly damp brush and smudge or blend the definite line between the colours.

CASTLE
(Plate 2-1 and 2-2)

Mix 3 parts White, 1 part Brown Velvet, plus 1 part Black Noir to make Taupe.

Use this to paint the castle, starting from the back and working toward the front. Shade each section as you go with Black Noir, then highlight the opposite side with White.

Using Cobalt Blue, paint the moat around the castle. Highlight with White. Paint the windows, doors, gate and flagpoles with Black Noir, using the No. 000 fine brush.

Add more Brown Velvet to the Taupe mixture and paint the roofs, drawbridge and road. Shade with Brown Velvet.

Paint the sides of the mountain with Brown Velvet, and shade the crevasses using Black Noir. Using a clean damp brush, smudge the Brown Velvet paint at the bottom of the mountain so that the colour fades away.

Paint two flags in Cobalt Blue, two in Bengal Rose, and the top flag in Lemon Yellow. Shade all the flags with a very small amount of Black Noir.

SMALL UNICORN
(Plate 2-2 and 2-4)

Paint the background legs with White. Shade from the top of the leg with Chamois, fading the colour out as you move the paint down the leg.

Next, paint from the neck down the body of the unicorn with White, leaving the head until later. Shade under the face of the unicorn with Chamois. Shade the chest and stomach area between the two legs with Chamois.

When you are happy with the shading, paint the head and mane in White. Make sure to go around the eye, so as not to lose it. Shade inside the ears and nostril using Black Noir. Carefully blend a little Chamois above the eye (like eyeshadow). Outline the eye and paint in the eyeball with Black Noir. Highlight the eye to one side with White. Refer to the Step-By-

enlarge as required

Step photographs M and N of eye and nostril being painted.

Paint the horn with White. Using the No. 000 fine brush, paint the lines on the horn with Chamois. Blend in the edge of the Chamois with a clean dry brush.

Paint the tail and mane with White. Using light, swirling strokes, paint over with Cobalt Blue, then Parma Violet. Wash and dry the brush, then gently blend in these colours. Repeat for the hair behind the hooves. Paint the hooves with Black Noir.

FINISHING

When the paint is fully dry, heat-set the design. Refer to the heat-setting instructions on page 16. Now you are ready to add glitter if you wish.

GLITTER (OPTIONAL)

Highlight the background mist with Glittering Silver and Glittering Amethyst. Brush Glittering Crystal over the rainbow and unicorn's mane. Brush some Glittering Bright Copper on the road leading to the castle.

Circus Clowns

(Plate 3: 1-7)

PAINTS

With this design, the colour of your garment will determine which colour paints should be used. You will be able to see from the photographs on Plates 3-1 to 3-7 that each garment has been painted in different colours, depending on the colour of the fabric. I will list the colours used in each section, which will at least give you an idea of what to use.

BRUSHES

Choose the size brush for each area of painting that you feel most comfortable using: No. 3 round brush, No. 000 fine brush, chisel-edged brush.

enlarge as required

PREPARATION

Make sure to have all the necessary equipment at hand. Wash the garment prior to painting to remove any sizing from the fabric. Do not use fabric softener. Enlarge or reduce the pattern as required, and transfer the design. Refer to the instructions for transferring patterns on page 14.

BALLOONS

Colours Used: Permaset White, Setacolor Bengal Rose (opaque), Lemon Yellow (opaque), Cobalt Blue (opaque), Light Green (opaque), Parma Violet (opaque), Cherry (opaque). Use any bright colours.

Refer to the Step-By-Step photograph O of the balloons being painted. Always start by painting the background balloons first. Use either a chisel-edged brush or a No. 3 round brush to apply the Permaset White over one balloon. Make sure to paint one balloon at a time — it will be easier to keep track of the lines this way. A reasonably thick coat of paint is needed in order to give a good base for shading. Also make sure to cover the transfer line with White. There is nothing worse than seeing the transfer line on the outside of the paint.

Once you have covered the balloon in White, load your brush with the desired colour and paint a fairly thick line around the edge of the white balloon. Wash and dry the brush. Then, using a semi-circular movement, gradually bring the colour into the centre. The idea is to have a darker rim around the outside edge of the balloon, with the colour fading to almost white in the centre. You may need to add more colour to the outside edge. Alternately, if you have applied too much colour and made the balloon dark all over, leave it until it is half dry, then blend a small amount of white back into the centre.

Repeat for the other background balloon, leaving the centre front balloon until last.

Circus Clowns

enlarge as required

CLOWN FACES
(Plates 3-1, 3-3, 3-5, 3-7)

Colours Used: Permaset White, Setacolor Lemon Yellow (opaque), Black Noir (opaque), Cherry (opaque).

Using either a chisel-edged brush or a No. 3 round brush, paint the clowns' faces with White. Go around the eyes, eyebrows, noses, cheeks and mouths. If you are painting on dark coloured fabric, this will need a second coat.

Paint the inside of the eyes with White, leaving a thin line around the edge, so as not to lose your way. This will also need a second coat. Once you are satisfied with the white on the clowns' faces, paint the eyeballs and the line around the eyes with Black Noir. Highlight to one side of each eye with White.

Next, paint the hair with Lemon Yellow. Allow to dry, then apply a second coat. Paint the noses, cheeks and mouths with Cherry. This will also require a second coat. When this is complete, highlight the noses, tops of cheeks and the smile lines with White. Fill the insides of the mouths and paint the curve lines with Black Noir.

On most light to medium coloured garments, I paint the clowns' hat with Black Noir, which is a nice contrast to the other bright colours used. However, on the darker coloured fabrics, I use Bengal Rose, Parma Violet or Cobalt Blue instead.

Now paint the clowns' hands with White, and after a second coat has been applied, outline with Black Noir, using the No. 000 fine brush.

The outline of their bodies, and the stars and spots can then be painted in any colour. Generally, a second coat will be needed.

The clowns' frills are painted later using the dimensional paints. Refer to Bits 'N Pieces on page 00.

FERRIS WHEEL
(Plates 3-1 and 3-3)

Using the No. 3 round brush, paint between the lines with Permaset Bright Silver Metallic. Generally one coat is enough even on darker coloured fabrics. Paint the seats with Black Noir.

CIRCUS SIGN
(Plates 3-1 and 3-5)

The sign can be painted with a striped or plain background — the choice is yours. I like to use Permaset Gold Lustre either on its own, or teamed with a Cobalt Blue or Parma Violet stripe. Paint the lettering with Black Noir. Allow to dry, then give all colours a second coat.

If you are including flags with the sign, paint the hanging flags with Setacolor paints, using any bright colours. Paint the other flags later, with the dimensional paints.

REARING HORSE
(Plate 3-4)

Colours Used: Permaset White, Setacolor Chamois (opaque), Black Noir (opaque), Parma Violet (opaque), Bengal Rose (opaque), Permaset Gold Lustre.

Paint tent background with Parma Violet. Allow to dry and apply second coat.

Paint the horse's head with White, shading inside the ear and around the bridle with Chamois. Continue to paint the rest of the horse with White, shading the cheek and mane with Chamois.

Shade the background legs with Chamois, blending in a little Black Noir towards the top of the leg for greater emphasis. Paint the hooves with Black Noir, then highlight with a little White.

Using Permaset Gold Lustre, paint the saddle blanket, feather, reins, sand and the curves on the front of the arena. Allow to dry and apply a second coat. Paint the rest of the arena in Bengal Rose, allow to dry and apply a second coat.

ELEPHANT
(Plates 3-2 and 3-6)

Colours Used: Mix Grey using 2 parts Permaset White

to 1 part Black Noir (opaque), Setacolor Bengal Rose (opaque), Parma Violet (opaque), Permaset Gold Lustre.

Paint the background of the tent with Black Noir. Paint the elephant's head with Grey. Shade the background ear and the folds of the trunk with Black Noir. Continue painting with Grey down the elephant. Paint the stomach, back legs and rear end first. Shade under the front leg and under the belly with Black Noir. Paint the front leg, up to the ear with Grey. Shade under the ear with Black Noir. Paint the other front leg (in the background) with Grey, then shade with Black Noir.

Paint the front ear with Grey, shading a crease line down the middle with Black Noir. Paint the tusks and nails in White.

Paint the headdress with Gold Lustre and White. Paint the elephant's stand in a combination of Gold Lustre, Bengal Rose and Parma Violet. When the paint is dry, apply a second coat.

FINISHING

The garment should be left to dry for as long as possible, then heat-set as described on page 16, before adding the dimensional paints.

ADDING DIMENSIONAL PAINTS

Now for the fun part! Feel free to use any colours you like — the brighter, the better. Refer to page 9 for information on dimensional paints.

Fireworks: Using Scribbles Glittering Gold, squeeze a thick line of paint over the transferred lines on the shoulders. Brush these lines down, spreading the paint out. Repeat with Glittering Starlight Rose, placing it between the Gold lines.

Squeeze lines of Glittering Gold over the fireworks. Do not brush these down! In the centre of the fireworks, squeeze a blob of Glittering Gold. Holding the bottle on a 45 degree angle, drag the tip, bringing it into a vertical position quickly, then lift it off. The result should resemble a tadpole shape, and can be as

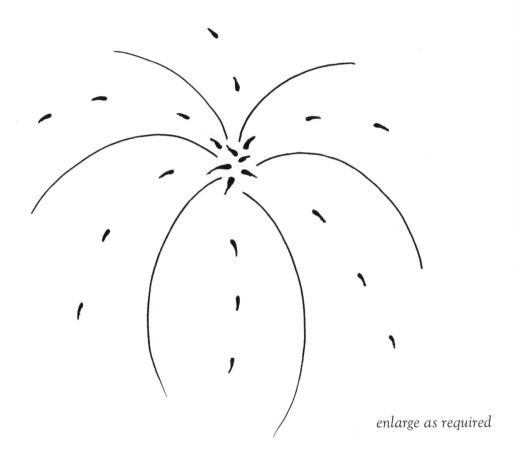

enlarge as required

small or as large as you wish. Place a few in the centre of the fireworks and some descending between the gold lines. Repeat on the opposite shoulder using different coloured glitters.

Flags: Paint all remaining unpainted flags with any bright, shiny or iridescent colours from the Scribbles range. Be sure that the nib of the bottle is always in contact with the fabric on which you are painting. This will ensure the paint does not lift at a later date.

Tent: Using Scribbles paints in the desired colours, paint the lines of the tent starting from the top and working downward. Make sure to keep the nib on the material. Apply constant pressure with your fingers and move at a smooth, regular pace. This will help to keep the lines even. Whenever you release the pressure on the bottle, shake it, tip down, a couple of times. This will keep the air away from the tip and help prevent the paint from 'spitting'. Have a practice run first on a piece of rag.

BITS 'N PIECES

Outline the ferris wheel with Glittering Silver. Squeeze blobs of Glittering Silver around the wheel where you want the diamantes. Push the stones into the paint to hold them in place.

Paint black Scribble lines for the flags to hang on.

Outline the word 'Circus' with Glittering Gold. Paint around the outside of the circus sign with Glittering Gold also.

Paint the clowns' frills. Shiny White, Shiny Purple and Iridescent Watermelon are among my favourites.

Brush Glittering Crystal on the top half of the balloons, and on the hats, nose, cheeks and neck frills of the clowns.

Using any Scribbles paints from the Shiny or Iridescent ranges, paint the clowns' eyebrows (using a different colour for each clown). Outline the clowns' hair with Shiny Bright Yellow.

Finally, paint 'criss-cross' stars with Glittering Gold or Silver, to fill any blank spaces. Paint some down the sleeves and on the rib.

INSTRUCTIONS FOR MAKING THE HAT

This is a very easy hat to make, so why not give it a go! Trace around a dinner plate onto a piece of paper then cut out to use as a pattern. Pin the pattern onto two layers of material and cut out. Fold one circle of material in half and mark with tailor's chalk 7cm (3") in from outside edge all the way around the halfcircle. Cut along this line. You should now have a hole in the centre. With right sides facing, sew both layers together around the outside edge. Cut a piece of ribbing 7cm (3") wide and 40cm (16") long and sew the two ends together. Fold in half, lengthways. Pin the seam of the ribbing to any point on the opening of the hat (this will be the back of the hat) and sew the rib on, stretching the rib to fit the opening of the hat.

Turn right side out and you are finished. This size will fit most children between the age of 2 and 13.

TO PAINT THE HAT

Colours used: Setacolor Opaques in Cherry, Parma Violet, Light Green, Lemon Yellow, Bengal Rose and Cobalt. Dimensional Pain Scribbles Glittering Gold.

Use the letters from the Circus sign and transfer onto the front of the hat. Paint each letter in a different colour. Allow to dry and apply a second coat. When the hat has been heatset outline each letter in the Glittering Gold.

Frogs in a Pond

(Plate 4: 1-3)

PAINTS

Setacolor Green Moss (transparent), Light Green (opaque), Gold Nacre, Black Noir (opaque), Cobalt Blue (opaque), Cherry (opaque), Lemon Yellow (opaque), Brown Velvet (opaque), Setacolor Emerald Green (transparent), Ultramarine Blue (transparent), Setacolor Fuchsia (transparent), Setacolor or Permaset White.

BRUSHES

Choose the size brush for each area of painting that you feel most comfortable using: No. 3 round brush, No. 000 fine brush, chisel-edged brush.

PREPARATION

Make sure to have all the necessary equipment at hand. Wash the garment prior to painting to remove any sizing from the fabric. Do not use fabric softener. Enlarge or reduce the pattern as required, and transfer the design. Refer to the instructions for transferring patterns on page 14.

enlarge as required

COLOURWASH BACKGROUND

To paint the colourwash background, refer to the instructions on page 27. Use Emerald Green for the lower section and Ultramarine Blue for the sky. If you have other shades of blue or green, use these.

LEAPING FROG

(Plates 4-1 and 4-3)

Use the following instructions to paint all the frog designs. As a guide for placement of shading, refer to Plates 4-1 to 4-3, and the Step-By-Step photograph P of the frog being painted and Q of close-up of frog.

Paint the frog's face, shoulder and chest with Light Green. Shade the area behind the hand with Green Moss. Paint the rest of the frog in Light Green. Shade both hip areas with Green Moss, then highlight the stomach, fingertips and toes with Gold. Paint in the mouth with Black Noir. Fill in the eyes with White. Paint a black dot in the centre of the eye, then paint a black line through this. Paint the goggles in Cobalt Blue. Paint the hat in alternate stripes of Cobalt Blue and Cherry, with a Lemon Yellow fan on top. Shade around the edge of the fan with Black Noir.

DIVING BOARD

Paint the board with Brown Velvet, then paint Black Noir lines down the board. Allow to dry for a minute or two, then, using a clean dry brush, blend in the black lines a little. Highlight in a few spots with White.

LILY PADS

Mix equal parts Emerald Green and Green Moss and paint the lily pads. Shade underneath the frogs and/or flowers with Black Noir. Paint in the lines on the lily pad with Black Noir and allow to dry for a minute. Blend in the lines with a clean dry brush. Highlight the bottom edge of the lily pad with White. Refer to Step-By-Step photograph Q of frog with lily.

FLOWER

Paint the background petals in White. Shade with Fuchsia (transparent). Paint the rest of the petals in White. Shade again with Fuchsia, but this time, make the Fuchsia deeper around the edge of the petal.

CLOUDS

Pick up a little White paint on a large brush, and dab the excess onto a rag. Paint the clouds using a swirling movement. Wash and dry the brush, then pick up a little Cobalt Blue and shade the bottom half of the clouds.

Clouds can be a great cover-up if you are left with a water mark from the colourwash background.

VARIATIONS
(Plate 4-3)

For my son Ryan's T-Shirt, I reversed the frog on the diving board, and used only the top half of him to create a different scene. In this variation, the frog looks nervous as the other frog is about to land on him.

To paint the water, pick up a little Cobalt Blue on a brush. Wipe the excess paint onto a rag, then paint around the frog in a semi-circular movement.

FINISHING

The garment should be left to dry for as long as possible, then heat-set as described on page 16, before adding the dimensional paints.

ADDING DIMENSIONAL PAINTS

Colours used: Scribbles Glittering Silver, Glittering Starlight Rose, Glittering Aquamarine. Paint the stamens of the flowers with Glittering Silver. Brush Starlight Rose over the shaded area of the petals. Paint swirls of Aquamarine and Silver for the water. Refer to page 9 for information on dimensional paints.

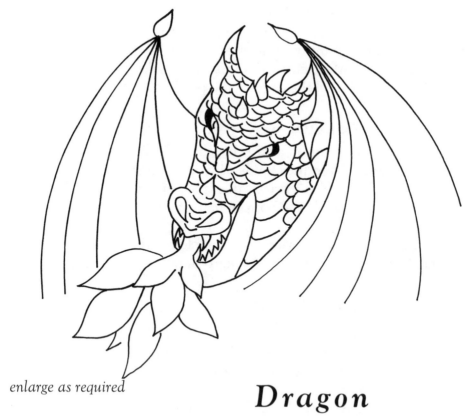

enlarge as required

Dragon

(Plate 5: 1-2)

The Dragon is the type of design that looks great on the front or back of a garment. I find the older boys prefer the designs on the back.

PAINTS

Setacolor Light Green (opaque), Chamois (opaque), Black Noir (opaque), Cherry (opaque), Permaset Gold Lustre and Permaset White.

BRUSHES

Choose the size brush for each area of painting that you feel most comfortable using: No. 3 round brush, No. 000 fine brush, chisel-edged brush.

PREPARATION

Make sure to have all the necessary equipment at hand. Wash the garment prior to painting to remove any sizing from the fabric. Do not use fabric softener. Enlarge or reduce the pattern as required, and transfer the design. Refer to the instructions for transferring patterns on page 14.

DRAGON

With the chisel-edged brush paint the background of the wings with Light Green, shading the area behind the dragon's head with Chamois.

Mix 3 parts Gold Lustre to 1 part Light Green and paint the dragon's head. Shade around the eyes, inside the ears and around the nostrils with Chamois. Paint the tips of the ears with Cherry, blending the red into the green with a clean dry brush.

Paint the scales of the dragon's face with Chamois. Allow to dry for a few minutes, then lightly blend the Chamois. You only need to take the sharpness off the scales. If you don't feel confident enough to paint the scales freehand, paint one scale and shade it, before moving to the next scale.

Paint the eyes and nostrils with Cherry. Shade the inner eye and nostril with Black Noir. Outline and paint the slits in the eyes with Black Noir, using a No. 000 fine brush.

Paint the horns with Gold Lustre, shading around each one with Chamois.

Using the green mixture, paint the neck, shading under the jawline with Chamois. Highlight down the front with Gold Lustre. Paint the scales on the neck as you did with the face.

Now paint the wings, one section at a time, using the green mixture. Take the paint two-thirds of the way down the section. Wash and dry the brush then apply textile medium to the last third. Keep moving the paint down into the textile medium until the colour has faded out. Highlight the left side with Gold Lustre, and paint a line on the right side edge with Cherry. Repeat all sections of wing until both wings are complete. Paint tips of wings with Gold Lustre.

Paint the teeth with Permaset White. Allow to dry and apply a second coat if needed. Paint the inside of the mouth with Black Noir.

FIRE

Paint the red areas of the fire, then paint the tips of the flames with Gold Lustre. Blend the two colours together with a clean dry brush.

FINISHING

Allow to dry, then heat-set, referring to the instructions on page 16.

Giraffe

(Plate 6)

PAINTS

Setacolor Fawn, Chamois (opaque), Sienna (opaque), White, Black Noir (opaque).

BRUSHES

Choose the size brush for each area of painting that you feel most comfortable using: No. 3 round brush, No. 000 fine brush, chisel-edged brush.

PREPARATION

Make sure to have all the necessary equipment at hand. Wash the garment prior to painting to remove any sizing from the fabric. Do not use fabric softener. Enlarge or reduce the pattern as required, and transfer the design. Refer to the instructions for transferring patterns on page 14. When transferring the pattern, shorten or lengthen the neck of the giraffe to suit the length of your garment. I have not included a pattern for the back around the neck, as all neck sizes vary. All you need to do is draw two lines corresponding with the lines on the front and add the spots.

If you are sewing this garment yourself, join the shoulder seams and lie the top open and flat to paint. If using a shop-bought garment, paint the front first and allow it to dry before painting the back.

Giraffe

enlarge as required

GIRAFFE

With the chisel-edged brush paint the neck area behind the giraffe's head with Fawn. Go around the spots, shading each one and behind the head, with Chamois. Paint the spots with Sienna, highlighting to one side with White.

Paint the head and ears with Fawn. Shade inside the ear, and around the eye and nostril with Chamois. Highlight the top of the ear, and around the eye and nostril with White. Paint the knobs on the giraffe's head with Chamois, blending the colour down into the Fawn. Paint the nostril with Chamois and shade in a little Black Noir. Paint a thin line with Chamois for the mouth. Paint the eye with White, and the eyeball with Chamois. Highlight to one side with White.

Using a No. 000 fine brush, paint the eyelashes with Black Noir using a curved sweeping movement. Paint the rest of the giraffe with Fawn, shading around the spots with Chamois. Shade the background legs and the stomach near the legs with Chamois. Highlight the front of the legs near the hooves with Chamois. Paint the hooves and the tip of the tail with Chamois.

FINISHING

The garment should be left to dry for as long as possible, then heat-set as described on page 14.

Autumn Leaves

(Plate 7)

PAINTS

Setacolor: Cherry (opaque), Fawn (opaque), Sienna (opaque)

Scribbles: Glittering Ruby, Glittering Bright Copper, Glittering Emerald, Glittering Gold

Permaset: Gold Lustre

enlarge as required

BRUSHES

Two household kitchen sponges.

PREPARATION

Make sure to have all the necessary equipment at hand. Wash the garment prior to painting to remove any sizing from the fabric. Do not use fabric softener. Enlarge or reduce the pattern as required, and transfer the design. Refer to the instructions for transferring patterns onto dark coloured fabrics on page 16.

If you are sewing the garment yourself, leave the side seams open and paint the front and back at the same time.

LEAVES

Cut two household sponges into eight pieces (one for each colour). Wet them, then squeeze out until they are just damp. Pick up some Cherry on a piece of sponge, then dab (do not stroke) the paint onto the leaves. (You might find it useful to put the paints on a tile). Repeat this for all the paints that need to be heat-set, placing the colours on the autumn leaves at random. I like to put all the colours onto each leaf. Refer to the Step-By-Step photograph R of autumn leaves.

FINISHING

Once all the leaves are covered, leave to dry then heat-set. Refer to the heat-setting instructions on page 14, before adding the dimensional paints.

Don't panic! The garment before you will look a right mess. My husband described it with one word: 'Yuk'. The glitter makes this design, so don't worry, it will look great in the end.

GLITTER

Squeeze the different Scribbles glitter onto a tile. Keep the colours separate! Using the damp sponge, pick up the gold glitter and dab it over the gold paint on the leaves.

Repeat with the rest of the colours. Each paint has a glitter that corresponds with it. Check the 'Paints' section above for the matching paints. When all the leaves are complete, outline some with Glittering Gold and some with Glittering Bright Copper. Do not forget the little stems and the veins.

Peacock

(Plate 8)

I absolutely love these creatures. The peacock would have to be one of the most beautiful birds ever created. We have five peacocks, one of which was raised in our kitchen. Harry or Harriette, as it has turned out to be, now resides on our back steps and watches every move made in the kitchen. Every now and then she pops in for a visit, but alas, she is not house-trained. So, back out she goes!

PAINTS

Setacolor Pearl Nacre, Cobalt Blue (opaque), Emerald Green (transparent), Black Noir (opaque), White.

BRUSHES

Choose the size brush for each area of painting that you feel most comfortable using: No. 3 round brush, No. 000 fine brush, chisel-edged brush.

PREPARATION

Make sure to have all the necessary equipment at hand. Wash the garment prior to painting to remove any sizing from the fabric. Do not use fabric softener. Enlarge or reduce the pattern as required, and transfer the design. Refer to the instructions for transferring patterns on page 14.

PEACOCK

Paint the peacock's head and body with Pearl Nacre.

Shade small fan shapes down the body, alternating between the Cobalt Blue and the Emerald Green.

Peacock

enlarge as required

Shade down the right-hand side of the neck and under the chin with Black Noir.

Highlight around the eye with White, making it an oval shape. Brush out a little black paint from the edge of the white. Paint the beak and legs with Black Noir. Highlight the top edge of the beak with White. Add a white nose hole.

Highlight the legs with white horizontal stripes. Paint the base of the tail near the body with Pearl. Shade close to the body with Black Noir, taking the strokes up into the Pearl. Using a chisel-edged brush, paint strokes of Pearl from the outside edge of the feather. Repeat until all the feathers are finished. Refer to the close-up photograph of the peacock on Plate S. Paint the crest on the head with Emerald. Shade in a few Black strokes for added depth.

FINISHING

Allow to dry, then heat-set. Refer to the heat-setting instructions on page 16.

ADDING DIMENSIONAL PAINTS

For this design I used Polymark Glitters, as the colours are irresistible: PM208 Blue Green Glitter, PM204 Bright Blue Glitter, Silver Glitter, and 26 clear stones or diamantes. Refer to page 9 for further information on dimensional paints.

Using a brush and the Bright Blue Glitter, paint all the oval-shaped feathers. Scatter a little Blue Glitter over the peacock's body.

Again using a brush, apply Blue Green Glitter over the Pearl strokes of the feathers. Paint lines of Silver Glitter over this. Brush Silver Glitter over the base of the tail. Paint lines of Blue Green Glitter over the crest.

Squeeze blobs of Blue Green Glitter where the diamantes are to be positioned. There are eight in the crest. Push the stones into the glitter. The stones will stay in place, so long as the garment is hand-washed.

enlarge as required

Mushrooms & Toadstools

(Plate 9: 1-2)

I picked up the cream fleece for this top as a remnant piece. As I could not match it with a cream rib, I used apricot instead. I then made leggings and lined a hat with the apricot as well. My daughter, Elyse, now has a complete outfit.

The fairy has been painted in orange and pink to tone in with the rib. An alternative could be to paint the fairy in mauve and pink and match with mauve ribbing. This is a great way to tie in a contrast rib with the garment you are making. I have included the pattern and instructions for the hat on page 76.

PAINTS

Flesh, Setacolor Cherry (opaque), Black Noir
(opaque), Cobalt Blue (opaque), Brown Velvet
(opaque), Fuchsia (transparent), Bright Orange (transparent), Green Moss (transparent), Permaset: White,
Gold Lustre (or Setacolor Gold Nacre).

BRUSHES

Choose the size brush for each area of painting that
you feel most comfortable using: No. 3 round brush,
No. 000 fine brush, chisel-edged brush.

PREPARATION

Make sure to have all the necessary equipment at
hand. Wash the garment prior to painting to remove
any sizing from the fabric. Do not use fabric softener.
Enlarge or reduce the pattern as required, and transfer
the design. Refer to the instructions for transferring
patterns on page 14.

BACKGROUND LEAVES

Mix 2 parts White to 1 part Green Moss and paint all
the main leaves. Shade to one side of the leaves with
straight Green Moss. Using a clean dry chisel-edged
brush, pick up a little green paint mixture. Dab excess
paint onto a rag. Smudge in the background leaves,
behind and in front of the mushroom and fairy.

    Once the leaves are complete, dry off with a
hairdryer so that the fairy can be painted straight
away.

FAIRY

Refer to Step-By-Step photograph T showing fairy and
fairy dress being painted.

Face: Using a No. 3 round brush, paint the face with
Flesh, leaving the eyes and a small dot for the mouth.
Blush the cheeks with Cherry, making sure to blend it
in nicely.

    For the outline of the fairy's body and face use a
mixture of 2 parts Brown Velvet and 1 part Cherry.

(This mixture gives a more subtle effect, but straight Brown Velvet can be used instead, if you wish.)

With a No. 000 fine brush, paint a thin line around the fairy's face. Wash and dry the brush, then very gently blend this line in. You need a soft outline only, so make sure not to remove it entirely. Paint the eyebrows and a curve above the eyes with Brown Velvet. Remember to keep the look soft. Paint the nose brown.

Eyes: Paint the eyes with White, still using the No. 000 fine brush. Paint the eye with Cobalt Blue, and dot the centre with Black Noir. Highlight to one side of the eye. Paint a very fine line of black on both the top and bottom of the eyes. Then, very lightly brush on the eyelashes, using only the very tip of the brush and very little paint. Reload your brush after each lash. That is how little paint you need on the brush.

Mouth: To paint the mouth, use the No. 000 fine brush and paint two daubs of Cherry for the top lip, and a larger daub for the bottom lip. Wash and dry the brush, then remove the excess paint. Highlight the centre with White, blending it in gently. Place a small dot of Black Noir in the centre of the mouth. Using Brown Velvet, place two small curves on either side of the black dot. Blend this in a little.

Arms and Legs: Paint the arm with Flesh, edging it with the Brown Velvet and blending it in as you did with the face. Repeat for the second arm and legs.

Dress: Paint the dress with Permaset White. Shade the Bright Orange paint from the bottom edge of the dress, upwards so that the colour is heavier towards the bottom. If the colour blends in too much, let the paint dry for approximately one minute, then add more Bright Orange where you need depth of colour. Shade in a little Fuchsia on the very edge of the dress as well. Make the Bright Orange deeper behind the fairy's arm.

Wings: Paint the wings with White, shading with Bright Orange and Fuchsia. The colour should be softer than the dress. Paint a line of Fuchsia around the wings, blending it in a little, to give a soft look. Paint in the veins with Fuchsia also.

Hair: Paint the hair with White. Swirl in strokes of Bright Orange and Fuchsia with the No. 000 fine brush. For the flowers in the fairy's hair, dab on Bright Orange and Fuchsia.

FALLING LEAVES

Paint one of the leaves with Gold. Shade Bright Orange over it while wet. Shade in Brown Velvet around the edges, blending it in with a clean dry brush. Repeat for the other leaves. For the curling leaf, highlight the curl with some Gold and shade behind the curl with Brown Velvet.

MUSHROOM

I can't help myself, I love mixing colours. Bear with me — these colours give the mushrooms just the right touch!

Mushroom Heads: Mix 3 parts White, 1 part Cherry and 1 part Brown Velvet. Paint the top of the mushroom heads with the mixed colour, going around the dots. Shade under the fairy with Brown Velvet and highlight around the bottom edge with White. Paint the dots with Cherry, blending in a little of the mixed colour to tone down the red.

Paint the under part of the mushroom heads. Shade in a little Brown Velvet over this area. Shade Black Noir into the part closest to the top. Blend it in well with a clean dry brush.

Mushroom Stalks: Add a brushload of Black Noir to the above mixture when you are finished with it. Paint the stalks, going around the windows and door on the large mushroom. Shade the right side with Black Noir and highlight the left side with White. Paint the line around the window and the cross bars with Black Noir. Paint the door with Brown Velvet, shading vertical lines of Black Noir down its length. Paint the door knob black.

Paint the wand using the No. 000 fine brush.

FINISHING

Allow to dry, and heat-set. Refer to the heat-setting instructions on page 16.

ADDING DIMENSIONAL PAINTS

Refer to page 9 for information on dimensional paints.

Colours used: Scribbles Glittering Crystal, Glittering Gold, Glittering Confetti, Glittering Starlight Rose. Prisma Glitter — these are glitter flakes that come in a bottle that you can sprinkle over the Scribbles glitter or suitable washable glues. It is also available from Duncan's.

Spider's Web: If you need to transfer on the lines for the spider's web, you will need to use a coloured glitter that will cover the transfer lines successfully. As I paint the web freehand, I use Glittering Crystal.

Sprinkle with a Prisma Glitter for a sparkly effect. This could be substituted with Glittering Gold, Silver or confetti. I would still sprinkle the Prisma Glitter over these coloured glitters as it looks great. In order to do this, the glitter needs to be very wet. Shade the Prisma Glitter all over the web area, then shake the excess onto some paper. Place the leftover glitter back in the jar.

OTHER GLITTER

Brush Glittering Crystal onto the wings, and the edge of the dress and flowers. Brush a little Glittering Gold onto the edge of the falling leaves. Add a star on the wand. Brush Glittering Starlight Rose over the top of the mushrooms and brush a little on the door.

Hat Instructions

(Plate 9-2)

Cut out the hat according to the pattern. With right sides facing, join the seams on both hat brims. Make sure to leave a gap for pulling through on one brim. Fold crown in half and pin at each end. Match pins to

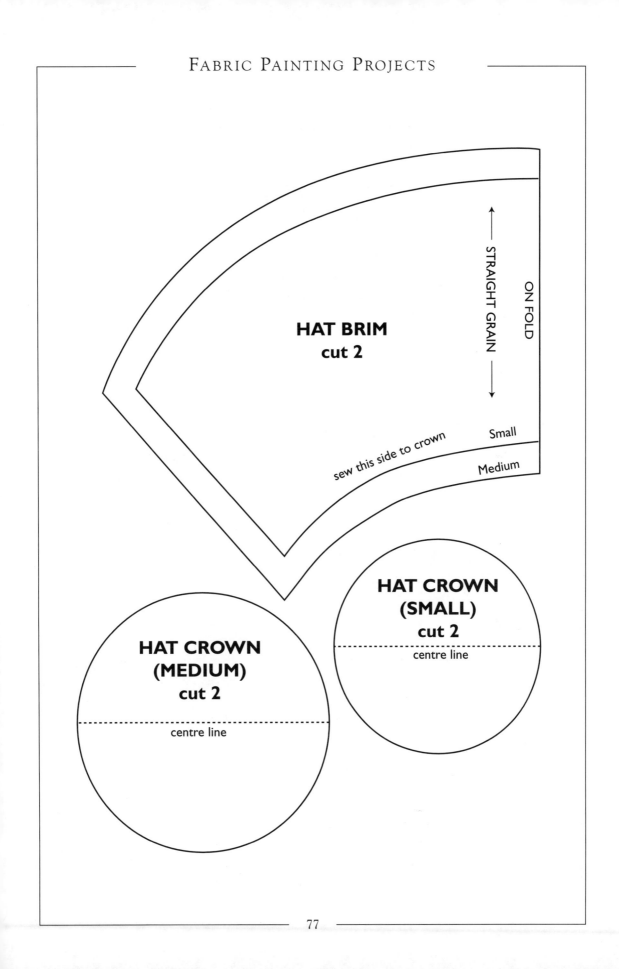

HAT BRIM
cut 2

STRAIGHT GRAIN

ON FOLD

sew this side to crown

Small

Medium

HAT CROWN
(SMALL)
cut 2

centre line

HAT CROWN
(MEDIUM)
cut 2

centre line

centre front and centre back seam of brim and sew together. Repeat for lining/inside of hat. Match back seams and centre front of brims, and sew all the way around. Pull the hat to the right side through the gap allowed. Press, then hand sew the gap closed.

Make the rosette by sewing a running stitch along the seamed edge. Pull in the stitch while rolling the strip of fabric into the rosette shape. Secure at the end with a few stitches.

It is a good idea to apply the Prisma Glitter before attaching the rosette to the hat.

Shoes

(Plate 9-2)

Brighten up a pair of cheap white sneakers to match your outfit by sponging on some Scribbles Apricot Nectar dimensional paint, and sprinkling some glitter over the paint while still wet. I substitute the shoelaces with strips of apricot nylon as a finishing touch.

List of Patterns